OXFORD
First Book of
Maths

Rose Griffiths

OXFORD
UNIVERSITY PRESS

OXFORD

UNIVERSITY PRESS

Great Clarendon Street, Oxford OX2 6DP

Oxford University Press is a department of the University of Oxford.
It furthers the University's objective of excellence in research, scholarship,
and education by publishing worldwide in

Oxford New York

Auckland Bangkok Buenos Aires Cape Town Chennai
Dar es Salaam Delhi Hong Kong Istanbul Karachi Kolkata
Kuala Lumpur Madrid Melbourne Mexico City Mumbai Nairobi
São Paulo Shanghai Taipei Tokyo Toronto

Oxford is a registered trade mark of Oxford University Press
in the UK and in certain other countries

© Rose Griffiths 1999

The moral rights of the author have been asserted

Database right Oxford University Press (maker)

First published in hardback 1999
First published in paperback 2000
This edition 2003

British Library Cataloguing in Publication Data available

ISBN 0-19-910982-6 Paperback

3 5 7 9 10 8 6 4 2

Printed in China

Contents

Numbers

Numbers are all around us.

What other things can you find with numbers on them?

- You can write numbers in words...   or with numerals.

Fifty eight

58

Which way is quickest?

This is a 2-digit number.

- Check that you can write every numeral neatly.

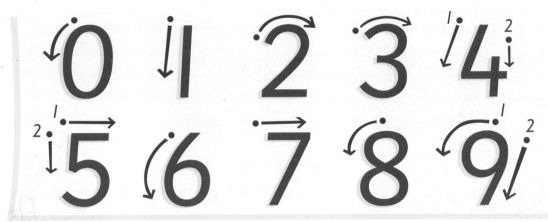

- We use numbers when we are counting and calculating...

How many zebra fish? How many angel fish?
How many altogether?

and when we are measuring.

Which fish is 4cm long?

- Sometimes we use numbers to help us tell things apart.

Come in number 5!

When I only have a few things to count, I count in ones.

● How many pencil sharpeners?

When I have lots to count, I put them in groups of ten, to make it easier to check.

● How many pencils?

43
4 tens — 3 ones

Ten, twenty, thirty, forty, forty one, forty two, forty three.

● Why do people like counting in tens?

The numbers we use today were developed in India. This is how people wrote them at first:

It's because we use our fingers to keep count.

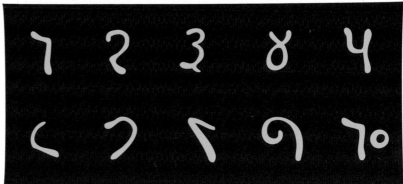

● Can you count backwards. . .

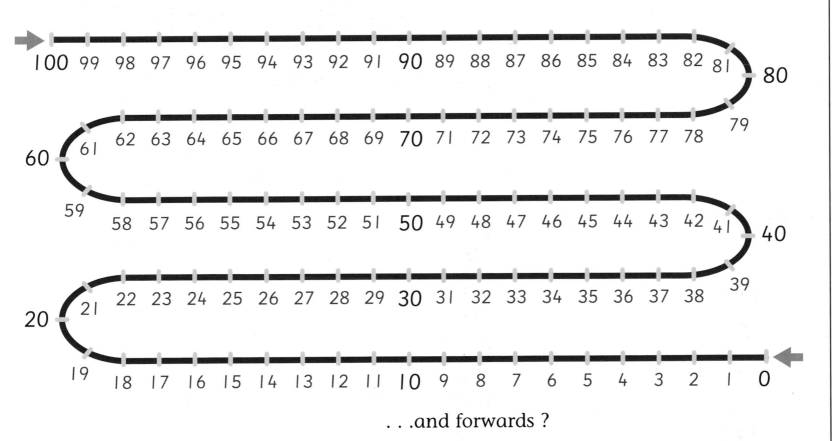

100 99 98 97 96 95 94 93 92 91 **90** 89 88 87 86 85 84 83 82 81
80
79
60 61 62 63 64 65 66 67 68 69 **70** 71 72 73 74 75 76 77 78
59
58 57 56 55 54 53 52 51 **50** 49 48 47 46 45 44 43 42 41
40
39
20 21 22 23 24 25 26 27 28 29 **30** 31 32 33 34 35 36 37 38
19
18 17 16 15 14 13 12 11 **10** 9 8 7 6 5 4 3 2 1 0

. . .and forwards ?

Practice counting backwards and forwards in tens or in ones on this number line.

One hundred, ninety, eighty, seventy, . . .

Sixty seven, seventy seven, eighty seven, . . .

Fifty two, fifty three, fifty four, . . .

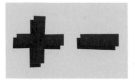 # Adding and Taking Away

3 lizards on the rock. . .

2 on the sand. . .

4 on the grass. . .

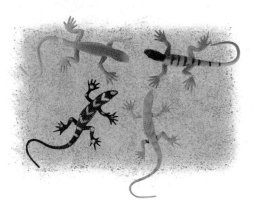

How many altogether?

Add up to find out!

2 + 4 + 3

4 + 3 + 2

You can add up in any order.

3 + 2 + 4 = 9

3 + 4 + 2

7 lizards on the grass . . .

then 4 ran away.

How many lizards on the grass now?
Take away to find out. **7 − 4 = 3**

● Taking away and adding up are opposites of each other.
Try these on a calculator.

● If you learn the answers to these questions
  off-by-heart, it will help you add and take away quickly.

2+4

4+3

5+3   9−6   10−6

6−4   3+6   8−3   3+4   9−3

7−3   8−5   4+2

3+5

7−4   4+6   6−2

How many do you know already?

Favourite hints for adding up.

Start with the biggest number.

5̶+̶1̶6̶
16+5=21

Split numbers up, then add them.

24+13
is 20+4+10+3
30 add 7 = 37

7+5+3

so

10+5=15

Look for tens.

2 4	1 3
2 0	1 0
4	3

Questions and Answers

You can ask questions in many different ways.

My friends' questions are all about adding or taking away. Can you match them to the questions in the middle?

I scored 3 then 8 then 6. What is my total?

What is 8 minus 5?

What is 3 plus 3?

What's 7 subtract 4?

I had 8 grapes. I ate 2. How many are left?

$$3 + 5$$
$$8 - 2$$
$$10 - 7$$
$$8 - 5$$
$$3 + 8 + 6$$
$$7 - 4$$
$$3 + 3$$

You are 10 I am 7.

I have 3 marbles.

What is the difference in our ages?

I've got 5 more than you. How many have I got?

Do you know all the answers?

- Some questions are easy to do on a calculator. Try these:

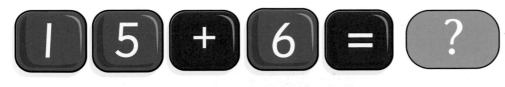

- Some questions are not as easy! What is the missing number?

Have a guess, then see if it is correct.

Is it 9? No, that's too big. I'll keep trying until I get it right.

This method is called trial and improvement.

- Can you find the missing numbers?

How many questions can you make up which have the answer 60?

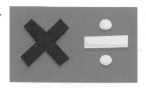 # Multiplying and Dividing

2 wings on each dragon.
How many wings on 4 dragons?
Multiply to find out!

Multiplying is like adding over and over again.

4 x 2 = 8

2+2+2+2

4 lots of 2.

Imagine I counted 10 wings.

How many dragons?
Divide to find out!

10 ÷ 2 = 5

Dividing can be like taking away over and over again. How many 2s make 10?

10 8 6 4 2

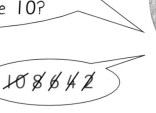

● Multiplying and dividing are opposites of each other.
Try these on a calculator.

6 x 2 = ?

1 2 ÷ 2 = ?

● Sometimes dividing is like sharing.

14 toads to share between 2 of us.

You can write it like this, too.

$$2\overline{\smash{\big)}\,14}^{7}$$

● You can multiply in any order.

2 × 3

3 lots of 2.

3 times 2.

3 × 2

2 times 3.

2 lots of 3.

2 x 3 = 6

3 x 2 = 6

What is 6 ÷ 2?

How many 2s make 6?

Which numbers are **odd**? Which numbers are **even**?

5 is an odd number.   6 is an even number.

8 is even.   9 is odd.

Can you see what is special about even numbers?

You can put an even number of things in pairs!

But odd numbers of things always have an odd one left over.

Odd: 1   3   5   7   9   11   13   15

Even: 2   4   6   8   10   12   14

● How many people?

Is it an odd number or an even number?

14

- We use ordinal numbers when we put things in order.

We came first in a 3-legged race.

- Can you see why we write these 2 letters after each number?

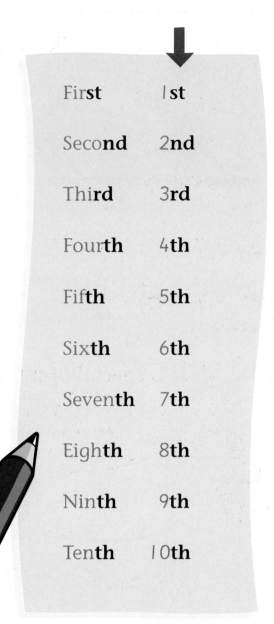

First	1st
Second	2nd
Third	3rd
Fourth	4th
Fifth	5th
Sixth	6th
Seventh	7th
Eighth	8th
Ninth	9th
Tenth	10th

- People use ordinal numbers every day, for the date.

My birthday is on the 31st of July. When is your birthday?

31st July

JULY

			1	2	3	4
5	6	7	8	9	10	11
12	13	14	15	16	17	18
19	20	21	22	23	24	25
26	27	28	29	30	31	

Times Tables

Have you started to learn your times tables yet?

Find a piece of card about as big as the dotted rectangle . . .
Cover up the answers. See if you know the 2 times table!

Try this muddled-up 2 times table:

Two Times Table

0 x 2 =	0
1 x 2 =	2
2 x 2 =	4
3 x 2 =	6
4 x 2 =	8
5 x 2 =	10
6 x 2 =	12
7 x 2 =	14
8 x 2 =	16
9 x 2 =	18
10 x 2 =	20

7 x 2 =	14
9 x 2 =	18
3 x 2 =	6
5 x 2 =	10
4 x 2 =	8
0 x 2 =	0
6 x 2 =	12
2 x 2 =	4
8 x 2 =	16
1 x 2 =	2
10 x 2 =	20

These numbers are called multiples of 2.

Multiplying by 2 is the same as doubling.

What is double 6?

Double 7?

Double 8?

Double 10?

- You need to know division facts, too.
  (They are like tables facts, done back-to-front.)

How many 2s make 4?

How many 2s make 8?

How many 2s make 10?

How many 2s make 6?

How many 2s make 16?

- Dividing by 2 is the same as halving.

What is half of . . . ?

20 2 8 12 14 16 18 24

- Your 10 times table is important too.

Do you know it in order?

0 x 10 =	0
1 x 10 =	10
2 x 10 =	20
3 x 10 =	30
4 x 10 =	40
5 x 10 =	50
6 x 10 =	60
7 x 10 =	70
8 x 10 =	80
9 x 10 =	90
10 x 10 =	100

These numbers are called multiples of 10.

Do you know it muddled up?

6 x 10 =	60
1 x 10 =	10
7 x 10 =	70
3 x 10 =	30
10 x 10 =	100
5 x 10 =	50
9 x 10 =	90
4 x 10 =	40
0 x 10 =	0
1 x 10 =	10
2 x 10 =	20

Do you know it back-to-front?

How many 10s make . . . ?

50 10 30 60 20 40 0 70 80 90 100

$\frac{1}{2}$ $\frac{3}{4}$ Fractions

We use fractions when we want to think about part of something.
Most people use fractions every day – especially halves.

It's half time in our football match.

I've eaten half an orange.

Half of us are wearing red shirts.

5:30

I'm 7½ years old.

I drank half a glass of milk.

My scarf is 2½ metres long!

You can have half of a group.
Half these kittens are ginger.

How many is that?

You can have half of a whole thing –
half a cake each.

Check that the two pieces are equal!

- You can find a place half-way between two whole numbers:

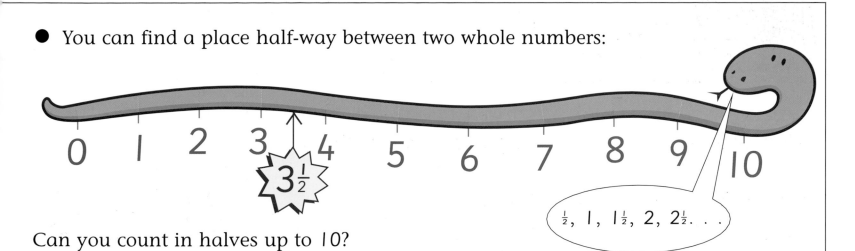

0 1 2 3 4 5 6 7 8 9 10

$3\frac{1}{2}$

$\frac{1}{2}$, 1, $1\frac{1}{2}$, 2, $2\frac{1}{2}$. . .

Can you count in halves up to 10?
Try counting backwards, too.

- You get half when you share things with a friend.

5 apples to share. $2\frac{1}{2}$ apples each.

- You can often cut things in half . . .   But not always!

- Halves are very useful. Sometimes we use other fractions, too.
  Have you used any fractions today?

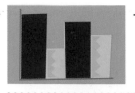

Facts and Figures

I like mangoes.

I like grapes.

We both like kiwi fruit.

A Venn diagram can help you sort things.

Fruit that David likes

Fruit that Shyla likes

Which fruits do Shyla and David both like?

Which fruit is your favourite?

● Alice can't decide what to call her mouse.

I'll ask my friends to help me choose.

No one liked Softy.

Tick the name you like the best

Bingo ✓ ✓ ✓
Gizmo ✓ ✓ ✓ ✓ ✓
Poppy ✓ ✓
Softy
Squeaky ✓ ✓ ✓✓

● Alice made a block graph to show what she found out.

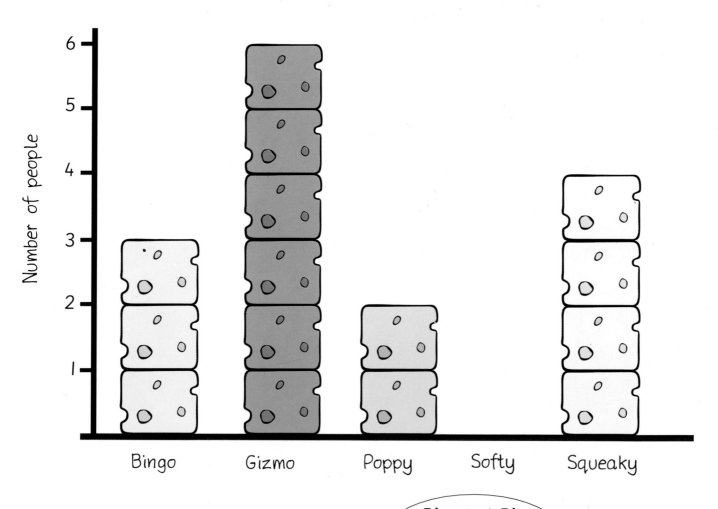

● How many friends did Alice ask?
Which name was the most popular?

I'm glad I'm not going to be called Squeaky.

21

Shape and Space

Have you ever thought about why things are the shape they are?

Why is the orange squeezer this shape. . .   and not this shape?

Think about the shape of half an orange.

Why are chairs like this. . .   and not like this?

Think about what would happen if a chair was not level.

- We use shape and space every day. Sometimes we need to think about where things are. . .

or how to fit things together.

- Shapes are all around us.

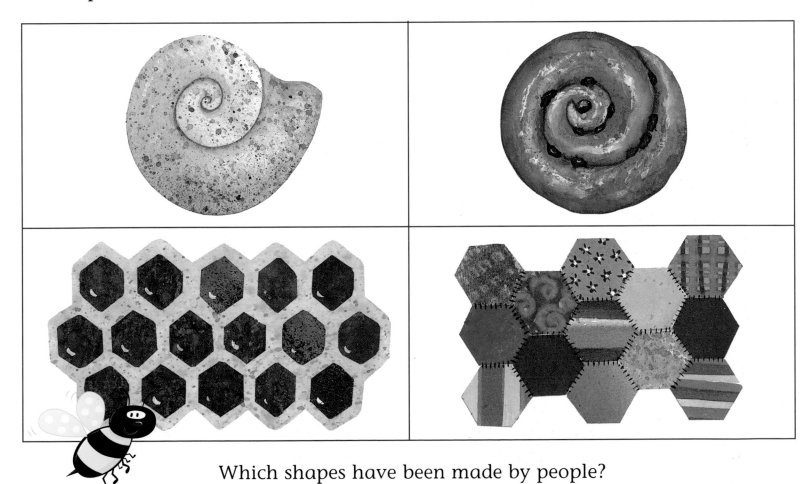

Which shapes have been made by people?
Which ones are natural shapes?

 # Position and Direction

There are lots of words which help you explain where something is.
Find the things we are talking about!

- The numbers on a clock help us explain which way something is turning.

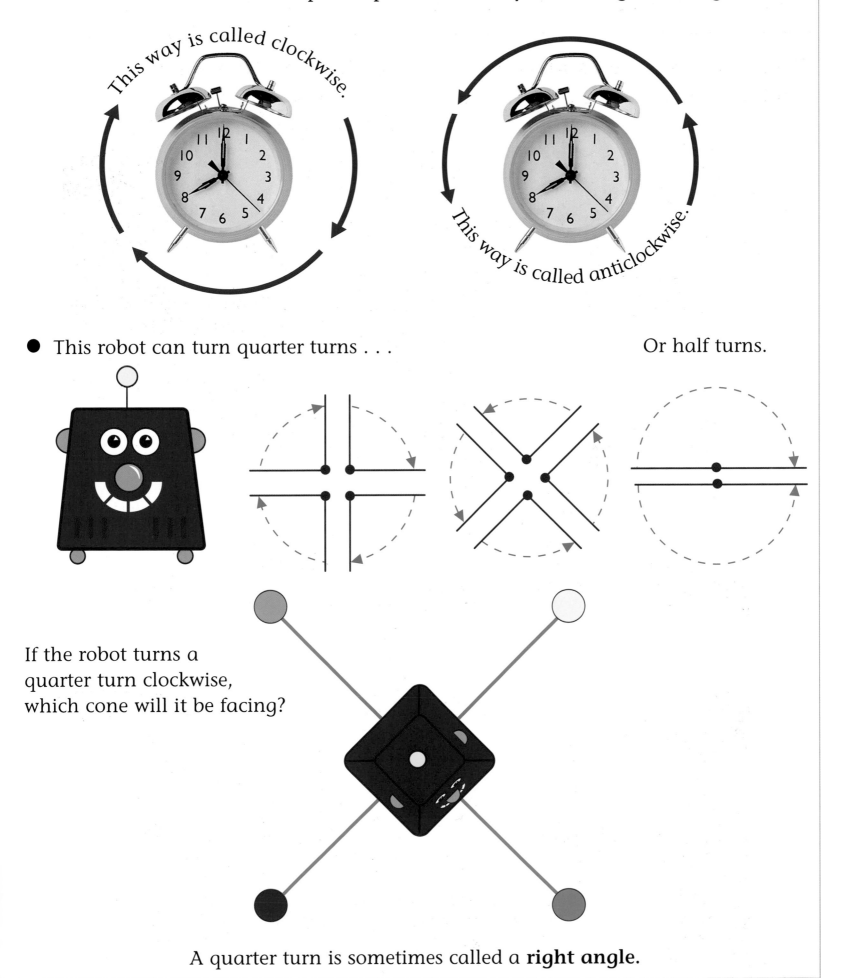

This way is called clockwise.

This way is called anticlockwise.

- This robot can turn quarter turns . . .

Or half turns.

If the robot turns a
quarter turn clockwise,
which cone will it be facing?

A quarter turn is sometimes called a **right angle**.

Drawing Shapes

I've drawn some shapes with straight sides.

Not like these!

Straight-sided shapes have special names, depending on how many sides they have.

- Triangles are shapes with 3 straight sides.

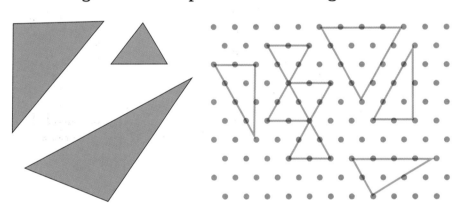 

- Quadrilaterals are shapes with 4 straight sides.

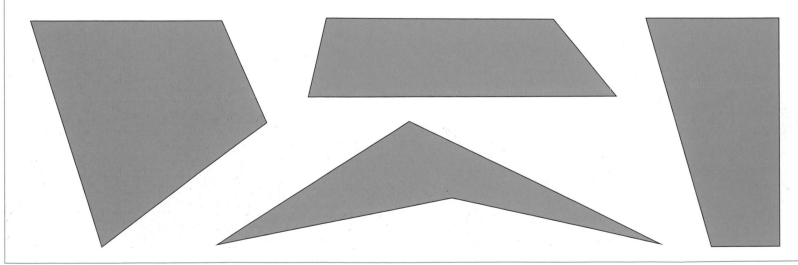

● Rectangles are a special kind of quadrilateral. They have 4 right angles.

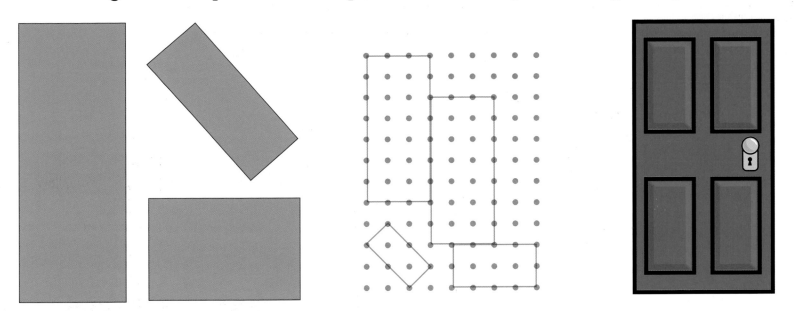

● Squares are a special kind of rectangle. They have 4 right angles, and their 4 sides are all the same length.

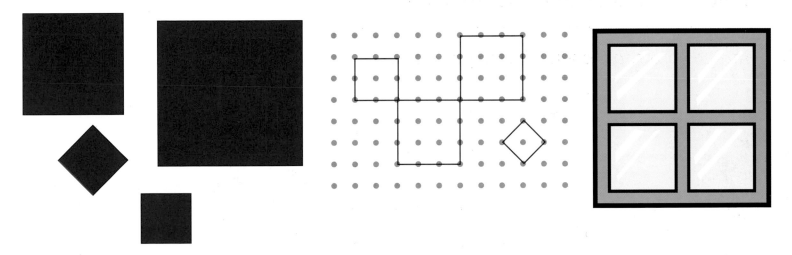

● Pentagons have 5 straight sides.

Rulers and Stencils

A ruler helps you draw straight lines.

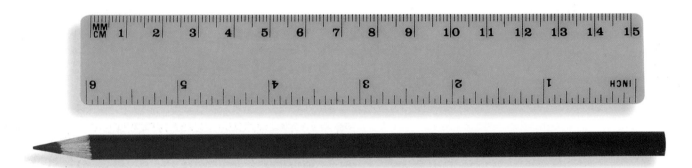

Can you draw hexagons and octagons?

● Hexagons have 6 straight sides.

Hexagons have six sides!

● Octagons have 8 straight sides.

Octopus means 8 feet.

Octagon means 8 sides.

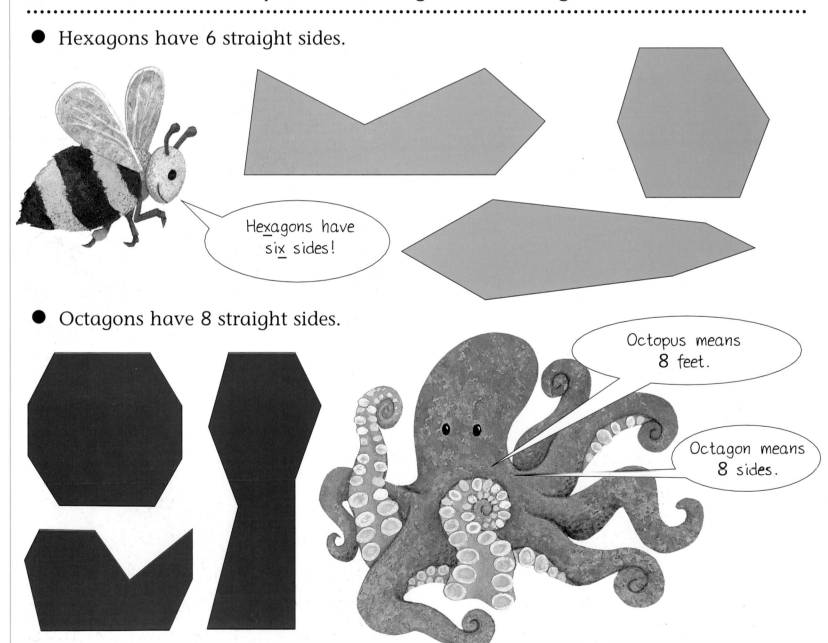

● These stencils help you draw circles and ovals

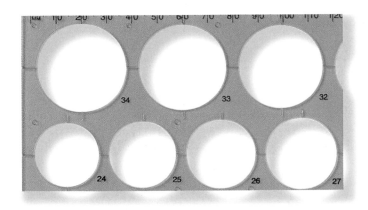

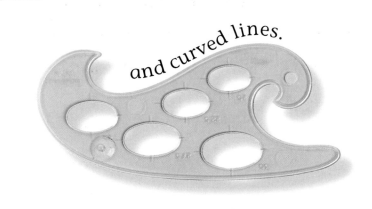

and curved lines.

Circles

● Draw a circle.

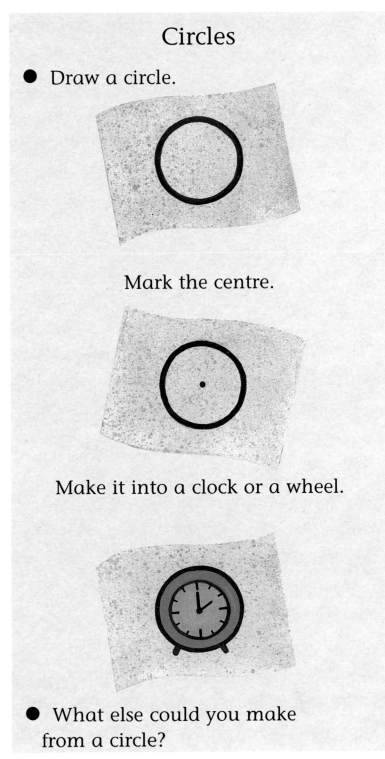

Mark the centre.

Make it into a clock or a wheel.

● What else could you make from a circle?

Ovals

● Ovals are a good shape for faces.

Eggs are oval.

● What else could you make from an oval?

Making Shapes

We can make three-dimensional shapes by cutting and folding paper.

Which shapes are we making?

Match them up!

A **pyramid** comes to a point. This one is a **square pyramid** because the bottom is square.

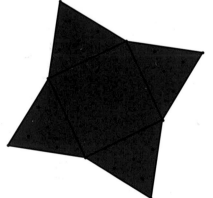

A **cuboid** has 6 rectangular faces.

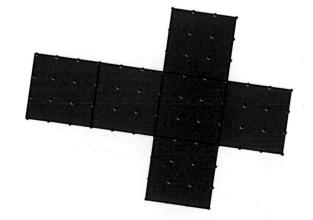

A **cube** has 6 square faces. A cube is a special sort of cuboid.

All these shapes have **flat** faces.

- It is harder to make shapes with curved faces. These shapes have special names, too.

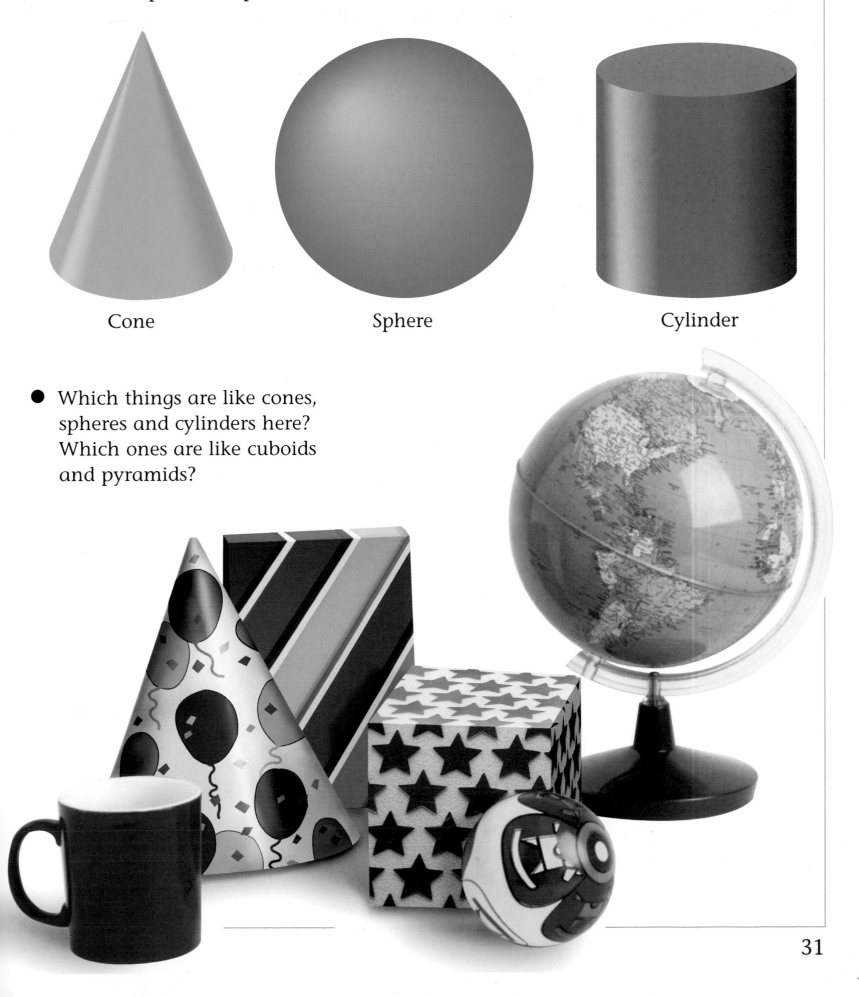

Cone

Sphere

Cylinder

- Which things are like cones, spheres and cylinders here? Which ones are like cuboids and pyramids?

 # Line Symmetry

If you fold some paper in half. . . 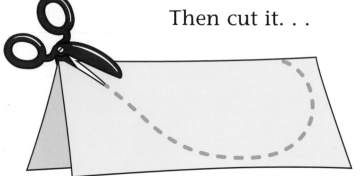 Then cut it. . .

You can make a shape with a **line of symmetry.**

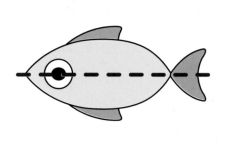   

Sometimes people call this line a **mirror line**.

Put a mirror along it, and you can see why!

● Fold some tracing paper in half, and draw a picture.

Open it out to make a picture with a line of symmetry.

Turn over and trace it on the other half.

Make sure your colours are symmetrical too.

● You can use a mirror to help you make a symmetrical pattern.

Look at the reflection.

Make this side match.

● This picture has line symmetry. Sometimes people call this reflective symmetry.

● Have you ever had your face painted? Which face would you choose?

Which two faces are symmetrical?

Patterns

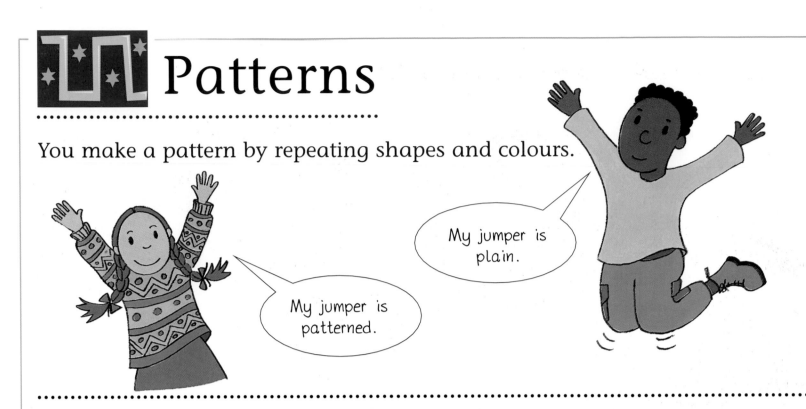

You make a pattern by repeating shapes and colours.

My jumper is patterned.

My jumper is plain.

- Some patterns are very simple. Some patterns are more complicated.

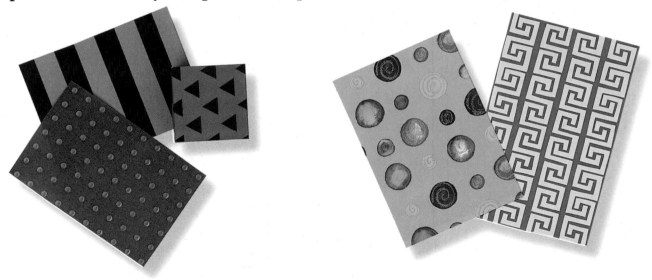

- You can make patterns by threading, sewing or printing.

● Can you see how these patterns were made?

Try making patterns in circles or rectangles. You could paint, or draw, or use sticky paper.

Building

Triangles and rectangles are important when people are building.

▲ Triangles are strong. ▬ Rectangles fit together well.

● When people are building they must make sure that what they make is the right size – not too big or too small.

● Could you build a block of flats, 4 storeys high?

● Could you build a fire engine with a ladder long enough to reach the roof?

● Could you build a bridge wide enough to go over the railway line?

● Could you build a castle big enough for a dragon to live in?

Measuring

You can measure all sorts of things.

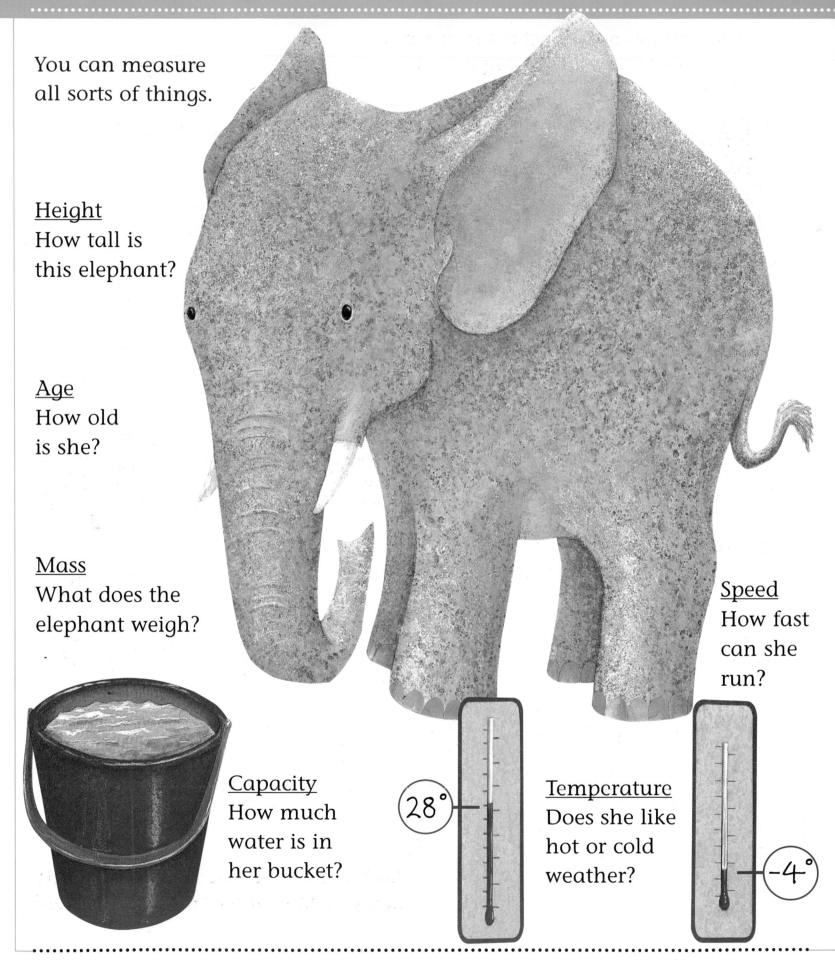

Height
How tall is this elephant?

Age
How old is she?

Mass
What does the elephant weigh?

Capacity
How much water is in her bucket?

Speed
How fast can she run?

Temperature
Does she like hot or cold weather?

28°

-4°

- We don't always need exact measurements.
  Sometimes we just want to compare things.

  She is taller than me, and she can run as fast as me!

  The elephant is younger than me, but she's much heavier than me!

- Sometimes we use more exact measurements.

  This bucket holds 10 litres of water (about 2 gallons).

  I can drink 20 buckets in a day.

  I don't think I could drink one bucket! Could you?

- Look at some bottles and cans.
  Can you find out how much is in them?

  2 litres

  2 pints

  250cl

  200g

  420g

  500g

  1lb

  Look at the labels on some food packets.
  Can you find out how much they weigh?

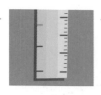

Length

When you measure how tall, how deep, how wide, how far or how thick something is, you are measuring length.

I'm taller than you!

No, you're not!

If we want to see who is tallest, we should stand on level ground.

- Do you know how tall you are?
  In some countries, people mostly measure in centimetres.
  In some countries, people use inches.

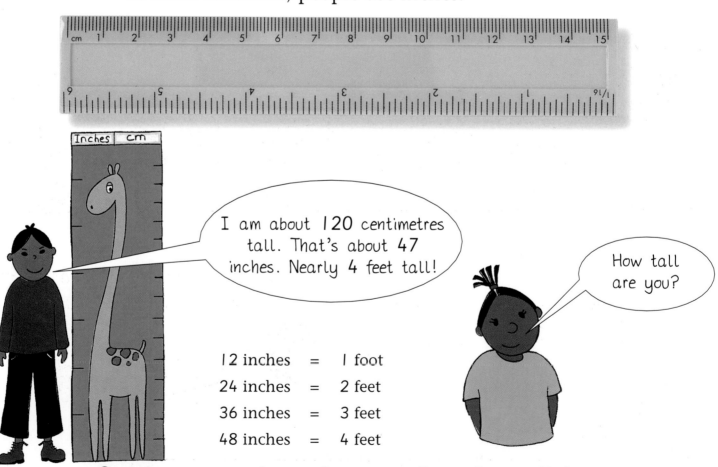

I am about 120 centimetres tall. That's about 47 inches. Nearly 4 feet tall!

How tall are you?

12 inches	=	1 foot
24 inches	=	2 feet
36 inches	=	3 feet
48 inches	=	4 feet

- Ask some people you know to tell you how tall they are.
  Do they use centimetres, or feet and inches?

- In the Olympic Games, people run races measured in metres.

We're in the 200 metres.

200m

- 100 centimetres make a metre.
Can you jump more than a metre?

0   10   20   30   40   50   60   70   80   90   100

Can you swim 5 metres?

3   4   5

Can you throw a ball into a bucket which is 2 metres away from you?

0   1   2

What else could you measure in metres?

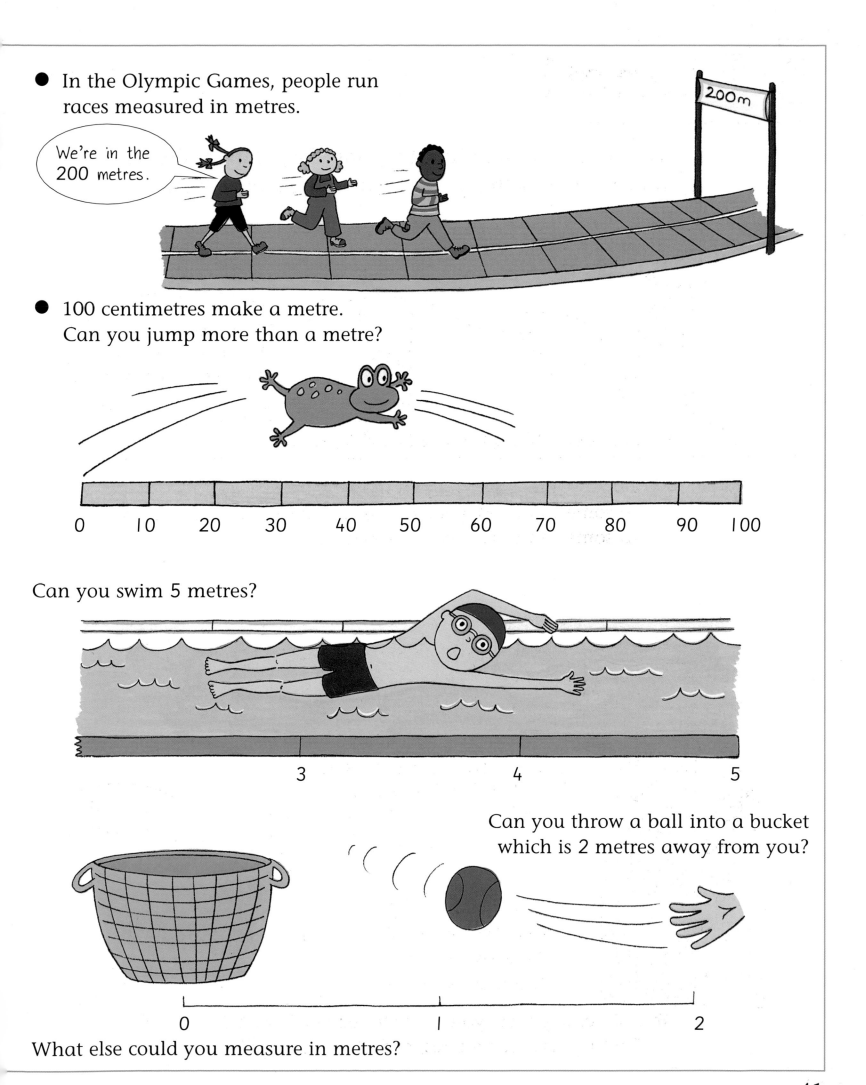

Time

Long, long ago, people invented calendars and clocks to help them measure time.

We write things on our calendar, to help us remember.

I've got swimming tomorrow!

● January is the first month in each year. December is the last month.

January

December

| January |
| February |
| March |
| April |
| May |
| June |
| July |
| August |
| September |
| October |
| November |
| December |

How many months are there in a year?
Which month comes after December?

● Babies grow fast in their first few months.

This baby was born on 1st March.

Here she is on 1st November.

How many months old is she?

- It can be very difficult to judge how much time has gone by. Sometimes it feels like time is passing very slowly. . .

and sometimes time seems to pass really quickly.

- A clock shows the time in hours and minutes (and sometimes in seconds, too). What time is it on each clock?

- There are seven days in each week.

Monday
Tuesday
Wednesday
Thursday
Friday
Saturday
Sunday

Do you know which day it is today? Which day was it yesterday?

43

Money

Most people use money every day –
when they go shopping, or if they buy
a bus ticket, or pay for a meal.

Different countries use different kinds of money.

- Most countries base their money on one hundred.

 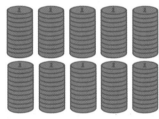 

One hundred cents make one dollar.
100c = $1

One hundred pence make one pound.
100p = £1

- If we only had coins worth one penny, it would take a long time to count 50p.

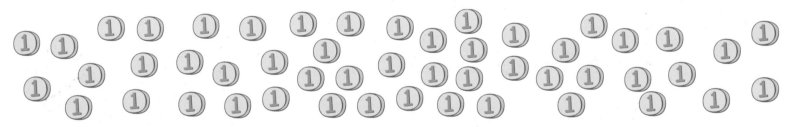

This is quicker. . .

and this is quicker still!

- Look at some coins and notes. Find out how much each one is worth.

Coins are made of metal, so they are strong. They are used for small amounts of money.

Notes are made of paper, and they have complicated designs, to make them hard to copy. Notes are used for bigger amounts of money.

- Make some pretend notes of your own, and collect some coins. Set up a shop and practise using money.

I've got £1.

How much change should I give him?

4 for 90p

3 for 70p

2 for 50p

Quick Reference

Fractions

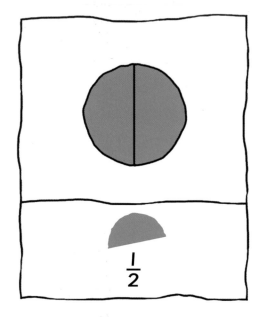 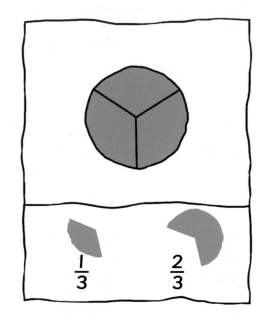 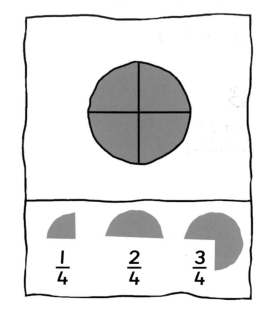

Numbers in words

Can you spell these numbers?

1	one	6	six	11	eleven	16	sixteen	30	thirty
2	two	7	seven	12	twelve	17	seventeen	40	forty
3	three	8	eight	13	thirteen	18	eighteen	50	fifty
4	four	9	nine	14	fourteen	19	nineteen		
5	five	10	ten	15	fifteen	20	twenty	100	one hundred

Time

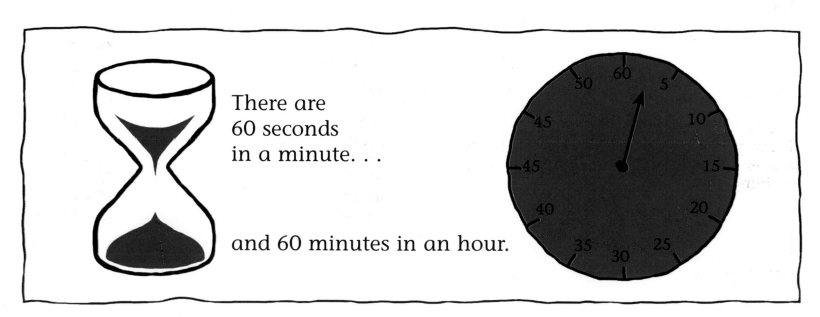

There are 60 seconds in a minute. . .

and 60 minutes in an hour.

Index

Index

Acknowledgements

Front cover illustration by **Larry Rostant**

Ian Cunliffe; 4b, 5t, 6tl, 7tr, 7c, 8tl, 8b, 10tl,11tl, 11b, 12tl, 12b, 14tl, 14c, 15tr, 15br, 16c, 16tl, 18tl, 18tr, 19t, 20tl, 21b, 23bl, 24tl, 25b, 26cr, 26tl, 27tr, 27cr, 27br, 28tl, 30b, 30tl, 31t, 32, 34tl, 36tl, 40tl, 42tl, 42tr, 43c, 44 and back cover tr

Sharon Harmer; 8 backgrounds, 12t, 12cr, 13tr,13b, 18b, 19b, 22t, 23b, 28b, 29b, 33, 38, 39cr

Su-Lynn Tan; 1, 5b, 6tr, 6c, 6br, 7tl, 7b, 8cr, 9b, 10, 11c, 11br, 12cl, 13tl, 13c, 14b, 15tl, 15bl, 16tr, 16b, 17t, 17br, 18c, 20, 21tr, 21br, 22b, 23t, 24, 26t, 30t, 34t, 36b, 37, 39t, 39b, 40, 41, 42, 43t, 43b, 45b and back cover bl

All photos by **Paul Bricknell**